IMAGES
*of America*

# BOGGY BAYOU
## Around Niceville
## and Valparaiso

IMAGES
*of America*

# BOGGY BAYOU

## Around Niceville and Valparaiso

Heritage Museum of
Northwest Florida

ARCADIA
PUBLISHING

Published by Arcadia Publishing
Charleston, South Carolina


Library of Congress Catalog Card Number: 2005926135

For all general information contact Arcadia Publishing at:
Telephone 843-853-2070
Fax 843-853-0044
E-mail sales@arcadiapublishing.com
For customer service and orders:
Toll-Free 1-888-313-2665

Visit us on the Internet at www.arcadiapublishing.com

# CONTENTS

# ACKNOWLEDGMENTS

The board of trustees and staff at the Heritage Museum of Northwest Florida would like to extend their sincere gratitude to everyone who contributed to this book. Many families, in both Niceville and Valparaiso, searched their attics and combed through their scrapbooks to provide photographs for this project. Thanks to all who were willing to contribute their family stories and images. Their names can be found in the photograph attribution key that follows.

The museum book committee—Carole Spence Apfel, Kay Harter, and Annette Brabham—were indispensable; this project couldn't have happened without them. Carole and Kay spent many hours contacting possible sources for pictures; Annette dedicated her evenings and weekends to scanning all the images. Mr. and Mrs. Cliff Brabham opened their home for committee meetings and were a constant source of support. Mr. Brabham generously provided the equipment necessary to scan the images for publication and tirelessly searched his own extensive files to contribute images he has either photographed or collected over the years. They are all advocates for the preservation of local history, and the museum is fortunate to have them among its supporters.

Over the years, Mr. Stephen Kent and the *Bay Beacon* staff have done an incredible job of recording local history through photographs, interviews, and their "Can you identify this photo?" series. They generously provided images and information from their files. Dr. John Q. Smith, Eglin Air Force Base historian, also provided photographs for the project and generously gave of his time to help with research questions. Adam Watson of the Florida State Archives was most helpful in supplying images from their collection as well. And thanks, too, to the editors at Arcadia Publishing, especially Lauren Bobier, who patiently led us through this project from start to finish.

All who were involved in this publication recognize the importance of recording the past, but one contributor's dedication made our own pale in comparison. The museum had requested an image of Mr. Claude Meigs from Mrs. Gayle Peters Melich, and in her last few days of life, she made sure the photograph made it to us in time. The museum thanks the family of Carlton P. Peters (Gayle and Mickael Melich and Stan and Sharon Peters) for taking the time to deliver the photograph during a very trying time.

All small towns have a history, but only few are fortunate enough to have residents with the foresight to preserve it. Both Valparaiso and Niceville are two such communities.

—Barbara A. Brundage
Museum Director

# INTRODUCTION

Although at various points in history, the Spanish, French, and British all laid claim to what is now northwest Florida, successful long-term settlement did not begin in Boggy Bayou and its environs until after Spain ceded Florida to the United States in 1821. And even after that, settlement came slowly.

This region, located just north of the Gulf and along Choctawhatchee Bay, is divided by a series of bayous, which made early travel difficult at best. For years, the only access was by boat from Pensacola.

Those who were willing to rough it packed what they could carry and headed east along Santa Rosa Sound, then traversed sandy pine ridges, palmetto groves, and longleaf pine forests to settle along the many bayous.

Pioneering in the Panhandle was difficult—not much grew in the sandy soil, and folks turned to other natural resources they found in abundance: the tall pines provided lumber and naval stores. The success of these industries, along with a national movement at the time encouraging responsible resource management, resulted in the establishment of the Choctawhatchee National Forest. This was the first national forest in the South, and it encompassed 376,000 acres of land.

With the onset of the Great Depression in 1929, the lumber and turpentine industries began to decline. Those who depended on the income from these industries had to find another way to survive. Fishing, which had once been just a way to feed the family, now became a source of revenue. A fleet of boats began to ply the waters of the Gulf for bottom fish such as snapper, grouper, scamp, and others. One market opened on the east side of Boggy Bayou, and a short time later, a competitor opened another on the west side. Fish were soon shipped by truck and by train to the New York market and then eventually to the world.

Other parts of the country soon became aware of this region as a "paradise" waiting to be developed. In 1919, development began, and soon the local lumber workers and fishermen were joined by folks from up North who were charmed by the "scenic beauty and healthfulness" of the bayous. The towns of Niceville and Valparaiso began to grow.

One historian has called this region the last frontier, since it was settled long after most of the nation. Today, however, tourism along the beaches and bayous and the largest air force base in the U.S. Department of Defense combine to make it a dynamic and growing community. Although this history barely touches the surface of all that has happened here, it will hopefully bring back memories of the quiet, sultry days gone by in the bayou country of the Florida Panhandle.

# IMAGE ATTRIBUTIONS

BB      The *Bay Beacon*
BGB     Mrs. Betty G. Blizzard
BJAE    Mrs. Betty Jean Aycock Edge
BP      Mr. Bill Powell
CB      Photograph by Mr. Cliff Brabham
CCB     Courtesy of Mr. Cliff Brabham
CH      Miss Cam Helms
CHS     Chicago Historical Society
CN      Mr. Lannie Corbin, City of Niceville
CPP     Family of Carlton P. Peters (Gayle and Mickael Melich, Stan and Sharon Peters)
CSA     Mrs. Carole Spence Apfel
CV      Mayor John B. Arnold Jr., City of Valparaiso
EAFB    Courtesy of the Air Armament Center Office of History, Eglin AFB
EG      Emma Goggins Collection
FBC     First Baptist Church of Niceville
Fe S    Mr. Ferrol Spence
Fr S    Miss Freida Spence

FSA     Florida State Archives
FUMC    First United Methodist Church
GEC     Mrs. Glenda Fay Edge Coon
HM      Heritage Museum of Northwest Florida
JG      Photograph by Mr. Jack Gardner
JM      Mrs. Jane Meigs
JMc     Dr. J. E. McCracken
JN      Mr. Jack Nichols
JP      Mr. James (Bud) Parish Jr.
LS      Ms. Lola Spence
LWL     Mrs. Louis Walton Lovell
M/CCB   Marthis Collection, courtesy of Mr. Cliff Brabham
NP      Mrs. Norma Phelps
TR      Mr. Ted Reeves
VB      Vanguard Bank
VFD     Valparaiso Fire Department
VR      Vernon Reynolds Collection
WH      Mr. and Mrs. Walter Hicks
WR      Mr. Walt Ruckel

This photograph of Gray Moss Point (in Niceville) was taken in the early 1900s. It perfectly captures the quiet beauty of the bayou region at the time. This land was originally homesteaded by George and Martha Parish and would eventually become the site of the Parish Boat Works. (VR/WR.)

# One

# THE LANDSCAPE

"Paradise"—residents of Niceville and Valparaiso are often overheard describing their communities this way. In both of these small cities, early settlement began along the picturesque shores of Tom's and Boggy Bayous. Homes and businesses sprang up where supply boats could dock and where graceful oak trees could capture cooling breezes off the water and provide relief from the hot Florida sun.

Those first choice lots remain prime real estate today, and many residents still enjoy the water view as they walk or bike along the old village streets. Today both cities offer all the conveniences our modern lifestyles require, and yet life here remains relaxed and pleasant—as if the land they occupy somehow retains its memory of the wilderness it once was.

One can only imagine the long-ago splendor of this untouched landscape. The Native Americans who first occupied the region found all the natural resources that they needed to survive. Excavations of local archaeological sites show that they took advantage of the abundant wildlife found here, and they harvested nuts, berries, and other wild fruits from the surrounding forests. Oysters, fish, and shellfish were plentiful, too.

In the 19th century, however, the remoteness of this region made it slower to attract more settlers than the rest of the state. A few hearty pioneers brought their families and their possessions here to settle along the bayous, but they struggled to provide for their families. The sandy soil was not as suitable for agriculture as they had hoped, and geographical limitations, such as too few roads and too many rivers, made purchasing supplies a challenge.

This region of northwest Florida would remain largely undeveloped until after the Civil War. But then, as the nation began to heal its wounds and war veterans searched for a new way of life, more settlers would arrive to stake their claims. Some became farmers or cattle herders. Others would come to take up the lumber and naval-stores industries, as new railroad lines made the wilderness accessible at last.

In the 1890s, James Perrine wrote, "The shore line of the mainland grew out of the distance as we swung out into the bay, following the channel. As things became more visible my eye was attracted by the wonderful appearance of a certain part of the shore. It was a riot of color and foliage. . . . It was a glowing jewel set in a group of lesser but beautiful jewels. We explored the country round about on foot and one and all agreed that it was the most wonderful spot human eye had ever gazed upon." (VR/WR and CB.)

Dr. Charles Mayer, visiting from Louisiana, wrote this description in 1919: "There is no mood of the water lover that cannot be satisfied at Valparaiso. If the mood be turbulent the gulf lies to the south. If it be peaceful the beach at Tom's Bayou is calm and the hard sand bottom is a joy and delight. To those who prefer the beauties of land to those of the sea there are hills and ravines, forests and wild flowers, sloping beaches and sheer bluffs: in fact, with the exception of mountains, Nature has supplied the Vale of Paradise bounteously with all that is necessary to satisfy every human demand." (CB.)

Even after settlement began here, the sense of wilderness remained. Lush glens, freshwater lakes, pure white beaches, and even wild animals could be found everywhere. (VR/CB.)

The earliest settlers had to rely on the waterways for travel, both for recreation and for trips to Pensacola to buy what they could not grow or make for themselves. (M/CCB.)

Shore Drive along Valparaiso Bay
Valparaiso Fla. (RM)

Even into the 20th century, the interior of northwest Florida remained difficult to access. For years, overland travel typically followed old Native American or early explorers' trails, and some local roads still follow those early routes today. Even though residents in 1919 were isolated from larger population centers, Mr. J. S. Mathis wrote: "Peace and contentment seem to be in the air. Everyone is happy and contented, even though they are the pioneers of the beautiful city to be. All have forgotten the cares and trials of the cities. . . . I am here to stay and enjoy the beauties of nature." (M/CCB.)

*The Moon Bidding its last Good Night to slumbering Nature on Beautiful Toms Bayou at Valparaiso Florida Taken March 2-1921 (RHH)*

After returning from a cruise on the bayou in 1919, another visitor wrote, "As the evening shadow fell we feasted our eyes on this semi-tropical jungle, where great trees festooned with vines and Spanish Moss overhung the placid waters. . . . There were birds of every kind— seemingly in hundreds, with their clear songs and calls, which with the splashing of a trout near us, we hardly noticed the approaching darkness." (VR/CCB.)

# Two

# NICEVILLE

In 1842, Jesse Rogers became the first to settle in the area now known as Niceville. According to some accounts, he brought a herd of cattle all the way from Louisiana and settled near Boggy Bayou. He would later move again to a location near what is now the town of Mary Esther.

By the time of the Civil War, others had made their homes along Boggy Bayou, calling their settlement, appropriately, Boggy. Many made their living by cutting wood to supply wood-burning steamboats.

Virtually all travel in the region was by water—roads were primitive to nonexistent. In the 1880s, all supplies were brought in from Pensacola by water, often on the steamer *Fritz*. Boggy was a busy maritime community by the late 19th century, with its own post office, general store, and boat yard.

The lumber and naval-stores industries brought prosperity to the village around the turn of the century. Logs were cut and floated down the creeks to the bayous, where they were sawed into boards for shipment to Pensacola. The community continued to grow around Eaton's sawmill along Bayshore Drive and Nathey's gristmill, located on what is Eglin Air Force Base (AFB) today.

As more roads were built in the early 20th century, the dynamics of life in the village began to change, and the importance of Boggy as a port diminished. When the Depression slowed business at the lumber camps, locals turned to fishing the bayous and bay first to feed their families and eventually to supply fish markets around the world.

In 1910, the community decided to change its name from Boggy to something more appealing, and they chose the pleasant-sounding Niceville. Not everyone agreed with this choice, and in 1919, it was changed again. The new name, Valparaiso, caused great confusion when a planned community called New Valparaiso developed across the bayou, and in 1925, residents decided to change the name to Niceville once again. There still remains a soft spot in the hearts of longtime residents for times past; occasionally one can hear them still refer to their hometown affectionately as Boggy.

Because Niceville was more easily accessible by water, the community's first businesses were located along the shore of Boggy Bayou. This is an early photograph showing the waterfront side of the village. The docks for the Turner Fish Company can be seen, as well as the home of Mr. Lud Givens. Mr. Tomberline ran the two-story mercantile store (center) and lived upstairs. After Eglin AFB was established, he rented these rooms to employees of the base. (EG/WR.)

The Nathey family, shown here, owned the first gristmill in the area. Mr. John Nathey later worked at the Bay Lumber Sawmill, which was located at the present-day Mullet Festival site. (BGB.)

Nathey's mill was located just north of John Sims Parkway on a creek flowing through today's Eglin Golf Course. Because Nathey's clients did not always have cash available, Nathey often accepted a portion of the grain as payment for his services. (HM.)

*launch Marie.S; Boggie Mar 1911*
*Capt Lambert Crawford*

The *Marie S* is captured here in Boggy Bayou doing double duty as a pleasure craft. Captained by Lambert Crawford, she was normally used to pull logs to one of the local sawmills. She was built at the Parish Boat Works in 1911. (JP.)

The *Anna* was built by Mr. Ruby Burdick for Mr. L. I. Smith before 1910 and was named for Smith's wife, Anna Durinda Brown Smith, and his great-niece, Anna Smith. It had two cabins and seats with leather-covered cushions that could be used as life preservers. The *Anna* was used as a mail boat for a while and then as a ferry and freight boat. She sank near Freeport in the late 1920s. (HM.)

18

The Lancaster family prepares the garden on their Niceville farm for planting in May 1919. Samuel Lancaster is pulling a plow guided by his wife, Elizabeth. Miss Al Lancaster Even is guiding a second plow being pulled by Molly Lancaster and Ida Lancaster Coon. (GEC.)

Samuel Lancaster and his wife, Elizabeth Edge Lancaster, raised seven children on their farm in the Rocky Bayou area of Niceville. (GEC.)

In the early 20th century, Grandpa Samuel Lancaster harvested rice from the bayou near his farm, which was located near today's Comfort Inn. He is shown here using a samp mortar made from a hollowed-out tree trunk to process the rice. (GEC.)

The Lancaster family also raised sheep. Grandmother Elizabeth Edge Lancaster, seated, is carding the wool so that Ida Coon can spin it into yarn. (GEC.)

This cabin, built in the early 20th century, was the home of Ansley and Ida Edge. It was located behind the offices at 962 John Sims Parkway. (GEC.)

This is the Aaron Howell family at their family home in Niceville, c. 1928. From left to right are (first row) Genevieve Howell, Norma Jane Howell, Aaron Howell Sr. (seated), Medford Howell (standing), Sarah Allen Howell (seated), Mabel Jean Howell (toddler), Ozella Phelps, and Leonard Olin Phelps; (second row) Jane Edge Howell, Ernie Howell, Sherman Howell, Lance Howell, Teller Howell, Alma Barrow Howell, Leonard Mansfield Phelps, and Mattie Easter Howell Phelps. The house was located on the hill across from what is now Bayou Plaza on John Sims Parkway. According to local tradition, Aaron Howell Sr. introduced the first mullet fishing net to the area and used one of the first mullet boats to fish locally. (NP.)

The Edge and Spence General Merchandise Store was located on Bayshore Drive and was one of the earliest stores in Niceville. Local residents could not only purchase groceries and dry goods here, they could also pick up their mail, which was carried from Mossy Head by horse and buggy. A reporter from the *Okaloosa News Journal* in 1919 wrote that he hoped to someday "go down to Mr. Edge's Store, sit out on the gallery, look out over the beautiful water view, and smoke up every dogon [*sic*] cigar Mr. Edge has in his store." The Methodist church first met in this building in 1913. (BJAE.)

In later years, the building was owned by Mr. Adolph Finck, who operated a bakery and grocery store. In 1934, most of downtown Niceville was destroyed by fire. The *Valparaiso Star* reported that the fire, although devastating, "had very little effect on the business life of Niceville. The activities of nearly an entire block simply concentrated in Finck's Restaurant, and business went along. . . . In it is found a post office, a wholesale and retail fish house, a grocery, a restaurant, a bakery, and the bay country's only draft beer dispensary, while the Niceville Masonic Lodge occupies the floor above." The building was located on the site now occupied by Parish Builders. (HM and JM.)

The house in this photograph was built along Bayshore Drive before 1920 and was the home of Burl and Mattie Parish Spence. This architectural design was used for two other houses in Niceville: one was built by Jeff and Arkie Allen, the other by Joe and Ema Marler. (JP.)

The Valparaiso Hotel (shown here in 1919) was the first hotel in Niceville. It was located on Bayshore Drive and boasted 14 rooms with electric lights and running water, notable features in this area at the time. The hotel was built by the Valparaiso Development Company. (M/CCB.)

24

Cebelle Warren Meigs ran this boarding house and grocery/café, which was located along Bayshore Drive near where the Niceville Paint and Decorating Center is now. Mrs. Meigs came to Boggy Bayou with her husband, Claude, in 1918. She was an accomplished pianist, and before her marriage, she traveled around the country giving music lessons. She also attended the Florida State College for Women. Many of the more affluent residents of Valparaiso traveled to her store in Niceville because she carried Monarch brand products. She typically rented rooms upstairs to teachers or to surveyors and engineers working for the highway department. In 1934, when this building was destroyed by fire, Mrs. Meigs relocated her Bay Hotel and Café across the street. (HM.)

At the end of the 19th century, this five-room frame building was the location of the Niceville School for grades one through seven. It was located across from where the Dairy Queen restaurant on Highway 20 is today. This school was consolidated with students from the three-room school on Glenview Avenue in Valparaiso in 1922. Mrs. Laura Parish, the teacher shown here on the left, and her husband were both lost at sea when their boat carrying timber to the Caribbean went down. (JP.)

Niceville High School is pictured in 1929. This school building was located on Highway 85 behind today's Edge Elementary School. It included grades 1 through 12. The building burned in 1926, was rebuilt by 1928, and was then destroyed by a hurricane in July 1936. (NP.)

This is the first graduating class of Niceville High School, pictured in 1930. Shown from left to right are (first row) Ola Howell, Myrtle Pippin, Virginia Barwald, Loraine Moore, and Vera Armstrong; (second row) Walker Spence and Sherman Howell. Note the picture's original caption, "Just Before Algebra Test." (Fr S.)

Until 1953, this school contained grades 1 through 12 and was known as the Niceville School. In 1953, Choctawhatchee High School was opened in Fort Walton Beach, and the white high school students from Niceville, Valparaiso, and Eglin were bussed there. Black students were bussed to Crestview. Niceville School then included grades 1 through 9 until Ruckel Junior High School opened in 1957. (CCB.)

In the 1920s and 1930s, towns of any size in this region organized hometown baseball teams. The Niceville team shown here played games in Baker, Crestview, Milligan, and other local towns. The team members have been identified as follows, from left to right: (first row) Bud Armstrong and Hub Erwin; (second row) Lee Reeves, Wilbur Senterfitt, Ernie Howell, and Joe Edge; (third row) Edward Webb, Ans Edge, and Jimmie Allen. (NP.)

The early commercial district of Niceville was originally established along the water side of Bayshore Drive because many of their customers came by boat. After a fire destroyed most of those buildings in 1934, new establishments were built on the other side of the street. Just a few months after the fire, the *Valparaiso Star* reported that the construction of a new two-story filling station near the intersection of the Crestview-Niceville Highway and Highway No. 10 "is in keeping with other activities that stamp this stirring region as one of the fastest growing areas in West Florida. We do not feel that any section of the state can show more private construction activity in proportion to population than is now to be seen in the bay country." Stores shown here in 1949 include Brabham's Department Store, Minger Brothers' Bar and Pool Hall, and the Niceville Post Office. (EG/CCB.)

The Niceville Theater, seen here in the early 1950s, was located along the bayou between the downtown area and Partin Drive. It was built on the site of Frywald's Theatre, which had been built by Mr. Edward Freiwald in the 1930s. At first, he constructed a pavilion to hold local dances. He later enclosed and then enlarged the structure so that he could offer residents the latest moving picture shows. His theater even included a Wurlitzer Little Theater organ, which could be played either manually or mechanically to add background music to the films. This was also the site where residents held a town meeting in 1938 to incorporate the city of Niceville. (CB and HM.)

# FryWald
## Theatre

### High Class

# MOTION PICTURES

Showing Every TUESDAY and WEDNESDAY—
FRIDAY, SATURDAY and SUNDAY
at 7:45 P. M.

## NICEVILLE, FLA.

In the 1940s and 1950s, the City Café was a popular gathering place for local teenagers. Many would stop by after a movie at Frywald's for typical teen fare such as hamburgers, hot dogs, and Cokes. (EG/CCB.)

Mr. Charles Brabham initially ran a dry-cleaning store in Valparaiso, but after World War II, he purchased this store location in Niceville. At first, the left side of the building contained dry goods and the right was a hardware store, but Mr. Emory Carr bought out the hardware store section. Cliff Brabham is shown here entering his father's store. (CCB.)

Beckham's Store was a shop for ladies' and men's wear in the 1940s. It was located in the old post office on Bayshore Drive. Beckham's later moved into a new store on the Valparaiso side of the bayou. (BJAE and CSA.)

The Niceville Volunteer Fire Department purchased its first truck in 1949, soon after the city installed its water mains. Shown in this 1950s photograph are, from left to right, Bud Parish, Randall Wise (mayor of Niceville in 2005), Joe Wright, and Sam Hern. At that time, policemen in Niceville were automatically volunteer firefighters as well. (CN.)

The first week of services of the First United Methodist Church of Niceville were held in 1913 on the second floor of the Edge and Spence Mercantile Building. Thirty-one people became members that week and were baptized in nearby Juniper Creek. Later, because the congregation shared a minister, services were held once a month in the Woodmen of the World Hall and then eventually in the schoolhouse as the congregation grew. In 1921, Mr. B. P. Edge and Mr. Sylvester S. Spence donated labor and materials for a new building, but it was destroyed by fire on Mother's Day, 1926. The congregation met in the Baptist church until the building shown here was completed in 1927. When this building was in the final stages of construction, the minister learned he would be leaving the church. He held his last service on the site of the new building, with those in attendance using blocks, timber, and other construction materials for pews. This sanctuary was replaced in 1961. (FUMC/Fr S.)

First Baptist Church

In 1910, members of the Goodwater Baptist Church of Christ in Walton County decided to establish a mission church in Boggy. The resulting congregation did not have its own house of worship until the building was complete in 1922. Rev. J. D. Hattaway, of DeFuniak Springs, served as pastor at the First Baptist Church of Niceville from 1921 to 1923. According to the church's history, he would walk all the way to Niceville on Saturday, preach the sermon on Sunday, and walk home on Monday. Church records show that members did whatever they could to pay their pastor: sometimes he received fish as payment, and once he was given a pair of pants. (FBC/CB.)

As part of the WPA (Works Progress Administration) during the Depression, a CCC Camp (Civilian Conservation Corps) was established in 1933 near the present-day entrance to the Eglin Golf Course along Highway 85. According to newspaper accounts at the time, it was the first such encampment in Florida. This photo captures the camp as it appeared in 1935. Four barracks, a mess hall, a kitchen, and headquarters served the men, ages 18 to 23, as they built roads, bridges, and buildings for the community. (CH.)

Five points was the name of the intersection in the background of this photo. The roads to Crestview, Eglin Golf Course, Bayshore Drive, and Highway 20 all converged here. This spot is now called the Niceville Triangle. (CH.)

Thomas Powell Sr. came to Niceville in the 1920s to work on a local sawmill. About 1930, he opened a store on North Partin Drive just above Highway 20. Customers could purchase food, gasoline, clothing items, or even a live chicken. Powell built the water tower seen behind the store. It provided water for the family home (at right), for use in the sink and to flush the indoor commode, a feature that few other residents had at the time. Powell's Grocery Store, pictured in 1932, was the first in Niceville to have electricity. (BP.)

Pur-O-Co Service Station, built in 1952, was owned by Walker Spence and leased by Earl Hutto. Hutto greeted everyone with "Fill-her-up?," and he was known as the "Candy Man" because he would give each child candy, usually candy peanuts. The parents got large Red Hots. In addition to pumping gas, Mr. Hutto would check the oil, clean the windshield, and check the tire pressure. (Fr S.)

It was a special day in town when the professional speedboat racers came to Boggy. The races were sponsored by the Choctawhatchee Boat Club, the Lions Club, and the Chamber of Commerce from the 1940s into the 1960s, but speedboat races had been held here as early as 1928. (CB.)

Lee and Laura Walton were the owners of Walton Grocery and Service Station, which was located on Highway 20 near where Hardee's is today. The family lived above the store, and their daughter, Louise Walton Lovell, delivered groceries on a bicycle that she still owns today. Students from Niceville High School followed a trail to the store to buy Moon Pies and RC Colas. (LWL.)

This Niceville High School building was built after its predecessor was destroyed by the 1936 hurricane. This school was the first in Okaloosa County to offer home economics classes and the first to include a lunchroom. The school became Niceville Elementary in 1952, when the high school classes were moved to Choctawhatchee High School in Shalimar. In 1962, this school was renamed the Lula J. Edge Elementary School. (BJAE.)

These cheerleaders from Niceville High School in 1948 are, from left to right, (kneeling) Betty Jean Aycock and (doing a back flip) Celia Edge Reaves; (back row) Pat Wymann, Quida Cox, Tony Jennings Brewer, Faye Metcalf Howell, and Betty Childs. (CB.)

Pictured here is a Niceville High School band concert in 1950. The *Playground News* reported on the event: "One of the finest musical attractions of the year was the joint concert presented at the Niceville High School last Sunday by the Niceville, Fort Walton and Crestview High School bands. The auditorium was filled and the young musicians were applauded enthusiastically." (CB.)

Having a fish fry has been a tradition in Niceville since the early 20th century. This photograph captures the Allen and Spence families enjoying one in the 1940s in honor of Ms. Arkie Spence Allen's birthday. Over the years, the community of Niceville has sponsored fish fries for holidays, political gatherings, and fund-raisers, and it continues the tradition today with its annual Mullet Festival. (CSA.)

These four businesses were located on Highway 20 between Kelly Road and Turkey Creek in the 1940s. The building on the left started out as a grocery store owned by Mr. Kelly. Lance Howell bought it in 1945 and converted it into a bar and café. The building in the center was initially a sporting-goods store and was later a flower shop. Mr. Ward's Barbershop occupied the right half of the building. The structure to the right was a barbeque owned and operated by Edna and Willard Alford. Doris's Restaurant, on the far right, was the place in Niceville where everyone who was anyone met to catch up on the latest election, fishing news, or any other current event. Folks flocked in for lunch, especially when the Fresh Mullet sign went up in the window. Doris's started in 1963 at the Holland Hotel at the Eglin Air Force Base East Gate. In 1965, it moved to the old homestead of Willis and Pearl Whitfield at 650 John Sims Parkway in Niceville. Vickie Cole took over the business when Doris Whitfield retired, and she ran it until the building was razed in 2004. (CB.)

42

What is now Bayou Plaza began in the 1950s with the construction of a Piggly Wiggly grocery store. M&K Drug Store (owned by Wilson Minger) was added, and then came Bill's Dollar Store. Three small separate buildings housed the "new" Ward's Barbershop, Wilson Minger's Realty, and a laundromat. The small buildings were torn down in 1970 to make room for a larger Piggly Wiggly and a TG&Y, and Skinners (a men's and women's clothing store) moved into the old Piggly Wiggly location. (Fe S.)

Chick Aycock and Del Richards operated a barbershop on the corner of Partin Drive and Highway 20 where the Magic Kastle Coin Laundry is located today. Mr. Aycock had previously worked as a barber on Eglin Air Force Base for many years. (BJAE.)

Groundbreaking for Okaloosa National Bank, the first national bank in the area, took place on April 24, 1963. This building was located near Hardee's and Turkey Creek on Highway 20. The bank was later named the First National Bank of Niceville and moved to the corner of Partin Drive and Highway 20. (Fe S and BP.)

# *Three*

# LUMBER AND TURPENTINE

The extensive pine woods surrounding the bayous had long been harvested for lumber and naval stores. According to an account of an early Spanish expedition, the first tar produced in the United States was made in Florida in 1528. Both industries would thrive in this region until a reduction in both the natural resource and demand would bring them to an end.

In the 19th century, early lumber mills were built along the waterways that lead to the bayous because they provided both power and a way to transport cut planks to Pensacola. The industry slowed during the Civil War, but after the war, new railroad lines gave the industry a boost by providing access to more forestland. The lumber mills increased steadily from 1880 to about 1930, but by then, over-harvesting had taken its toll. Production dropped, and mills slowly disappeared. Only three percent of the old-growth forest still exists, protected by the federal government on Eglin Reservation.

"Naval stores" was originally the term for products that were essential to the production and maintenance of wooden ships. Turpentine, a derivative of tree resin used in paint solvents, disinfectants, liniments, lamp fuel, and perfume; and rosin, used to make paper, soap, and varnish, also became important products of the local pine forests as well. By 1839, there were several turpentine stills located a few miles north of Boggy Bayou, and the industry continued to grow after the Civil War, as former slaves came to the stills to find work.

In 1908, Choctawhatchee National Forest was created on land that comprises today's Eglin Air Force Base. The forest, which encompassed well over 300,000 acres, was the first national forest in the South; by 1913, it produced $16,000 a year in timber and turpentine sales. In 1912, Florida provided almost half of the nation's turpentine products. Production began to decline, however, when exports to Europe were suspended during World War I, and by the 1940s, only a few small producers remained.

The Choctawhatchee National Forest originally included many old-growth longleaf pine trees, which provided excellent heartwood lumber and gum. At first, local homesteaders cut lumber for fuel for both the steamships and the railroad engines. But as the forest shifted to government ownership and the naval stores industry grew, many leased claims to run turpentine camps. A 1940 Forest Service bulletin announced that this forest "was the one area then under Forest Service control which supported species of pine suitable for the production of naval stores; consequently, it became the birthplace of Forest Service investigations in that field." In swampy areas, trails were cut from tree to tree to reduce the potential for workers to be bitten by snakes. In dry sandy areas, workers cleared pine needles and branches away from the trees to reduce the danger of fire. (FSA.)

F. C. Eaton built the first sawmill on Bayshore Drive where Lions Park is today. Sylvester Spence was the bookkeeper, and Burl Spence was the sawyer. The mill burned, and Mr. Eaton helped the Spence brothers relocate the mill to Turkey Creek at the head of Boggy Bayou. The Spence mill, shown here, was steam driven and employed a work force of 25. It continued to operate until the Great Depression. (HM and Fr S.)

Logs were floated up Boggy Bayou to the mill. They were kept floating in a holding pond located behind where the Coffee Shoppe is today. After the lumber was cut, it was stored in sheds along the west shore of the bayou until it was shipped to Pensacola. (JP.)

Until motorized trucks came into use, teams of oxen hauled timber from the Choctawhatchee Forest to the mill on Boggy Bayou. Oxen were often preferred over mules because their split hooves allowed them to dig in and move more easily over muddy roads. The team in this photo belonged to Matt Sweeney. (JP.)

This is a gathering of the drivers—both truck and mule teams—that worked together at the sawmill. Some of the drivers were Ed Cutchins, the Atwell boys, Johnny Whitfield, Willis Whitfield, and Little Joe Marler. Since the drivers did not own cars, they had to walk home after delivering their trucks to Burl Spence's home on Bay Shore Drive at the end of each workday. (JP.)

Trailers like the one shown here were eventually adapted to haul the logs from the forest to the mill. They were made by attaching the rear axle of a truck to a cross piece called a bolster. A shaft connected the trailer to the truck with a pin. The two men in the picture are holding poles that keep the logs from rolling off the trailer. (JP.)

Four logs were about all the trucks could carry. Most logs were about 30 to 40 inches in diameter. The dark ring around the edge of the log held the sap, while the rest was pure heartwood. (JP.)

When they reached Shirks Bayou, the men would pull the truck as close to the water as they could and then release the logs by removing the poles from either side of the truck bed. The men would then use their peaveys (log hooks) to roll the logs into the water. (JP.)

James Parish Sr. is pictured on the boat he used to tow logs from Shirks Bayou to the Spence Sawmill at the head of Boggy Bayou. Logs were held together using "dogs and chains," sharp wedges attached to a chain. The wedges were driven into the logs to tie them together. "Floaters" (logs that could float) were tied to "dead heads" (logs that did not) and were pulled along behind the boat. (JP.)

The Spence Commissary, shown here in the 1920s, was a general store for mill employees. Supplies were brought in by boat three times per week. Pictured here, from left to right, are Hazel Erwin, Elizabeth Spence with baby Francis, Sylvester Spence, Wallace Spence, two unidentified salesmen, Willy Spence on his tricycle, Harold McCullough, Anse Edge, Mr. Adkinson, Walter Spence, Miss Hudson, and Mr. Agerton. Sylvester Spence took care of the bookkeeping for the mill and often walked all the way to DeFuniak Springs to do his banking. (Fr S.)

Like most other companies at the time, Spence's Bayou Mill Company issued its own stamped metal coins. These could be used at the commissary or at local stores if the proprietors accepted them. (HM.)

Pictured here are a turpentine still, windmill, and water tower is Okaloosa County in 1920. The first known turpentine still in the area was built by a man named Ballentine. Soon others followed, and one run by L. L. Shaw became one of the largest. (FSA.)

In 1908, Congress set aside 376,000 acres of land and proclaimed it the Choctawhatchee National Forest. Its peak year of production was 1938, and at one time, an estimated 26 turpentine stills were in operation there. In June 1940, the forest was transferred to the War Department for use as a training field. (FSA.)

This photo, taken in the late 1920s, shows a worker gathering sap from a turpentine pine stand in Choctawhatchee National Forest. An axe was used to cut a large gash into the tree, and then a metal "apron" was pressed into the opening. Just above the apron, streaks were cut into the bark, and a container was suspended just below the apron to collect the sap as it oozed from the streak. As each wound in the tree healed, another gash was made just above it, creating the "cat face" appearance shown here. Trees were worked in the warm months, typically from March through November. (FSA.)

The still for processing resin was located in an open two-story building. The cooper's shed, where barrels were made to contain the finished products for shipment, was usually a separate structure. Larger camps might also include a wagon shed and blacksmith shop. (EAFB.)

This cooper's shed was located at Garniers Bayou in the Choctawhatchee National Forest. (EAFB.)

Turpentine still operators either owned or leased the forestland and were responsible for building the camps and recruiting workers. Many came from other states when the industry at home faded. Free housing was one incentive. Every camp had a few shanties for the workers and a barn and lot for the animals that worked at the site. Shanties were usually in rows, and each housed an entire family. Single men often shared one building. The walls were usually made from slabs left over from the sawmills. Interior walls were sometimes covered with newspapers. A fireplace served as both stove and a source of heat. (FSA.)

The *Swan* at the Valparaiso Dock ... Fla. (Feb. 2, 1921)

The *Swan* was a 60-ton, 100-foot vessel that carried naval stores from stills in the Choctawhatchee Forest to Pensacola. In the fall of 1926, she was retired from this run because the construction of a new bridge reduced the need for water transportation. For several months, she was anchored in Marcus Bayou, and during that time, Capt. Perry Helms or Mr. U. R. Hicks would start the engine once a month to keep her in shape. As they prepared to start the engines in April 1927, a fire broke out. It spread rapidly, inflicting serious burns on both men, who barely had time to escape. It was reported that smoke from the fire was so dense it could be seen almost all the way to Pensacola. (M/CCB.)

The *Captain Fritz* was built in Mississippi. As early as 1904, she made weekly trips between the bayous and Pensacola, hauling barrels of naval stores to the port city and bringing supplies back to the turpentine camps. Passengers paid $3 for the daylong trip from Freeport to Pensacola, including meals. One passenger's recollections appeared in the *DeFuniak Springs Herald-Breeze* in 1973: "[We were] raced to Freeport in the Maxwell touring car, madly blowing the rubber bulb horn for the last few miles so the Fritz would wait for us, scrambling up the gangplank with our straw suit cases, then settling down to a real Southern Breakfast. . . . Dinner was served at noon. . . . By early afternoon our voyage would end at Camp Walton where the Fritz usually docked at Buck's store to discharge passengers and freight and take on more." On one run, it was recorded that she carried 354 barrels of naval stores and three passengers. The *Captain Fritz* eventually burned and sank near Vernon, Florida. For years, residents reported that they could see her bulk above the water when the river was low. Regular steamboat runs came to an end when roads and bridges were built in the 1930s. (CH.)

The gentleman in this photograph is Captain Bell of the *Fritz*. (HM.)

# Four

# VALPARAISO

At the turn of the 20th century, much of the land along Boggy Bayou was still available to homesteaders through the U.S. General Land Office. Mr. Allen Brown Jr. settled here in 1901, but he died just a few years later. Few other settlers followed, until, in 1919, a Chicago businessman decided to develop the point of land between Tom's and Boggy Bayous and market it as a resort.

John Perrine thought that his carefully planned community would be easy to promote, since the area was rich in natural assets such as white sandy beaches, excellent fishing and hunting opportunities, and pristine rivers and streams. Perrine hoped that his village in the midst of all this natural beauty would lure investors seeking to escape the cold Northern winters.

According to an article in the *Milton Gazette* in January 1922, Perrine's "Vale of Paradise" boasted "miles of paved streets [actually hard-surfaced clay], electric lights, telephone, cement sidewalks, and about one hundred beautiful bungalows." The article goes on to say that Mr. Perrine had just passed away "from overwork and exhaustion." His dream would have to be realized by another enthusiastic entrepreneur.

That year, fellow Chicagoan James E. Plew purchased Perrine's development company and built an inn, a golf course, a bank, and a winery, sparing no expense to make the community grow. In 1920, there had been only two commercial buildings in Valparaiso: Perrine's Office of the Valparaiso Development Company and the Bay Shore Hotel. By the mid-1920s, under Plew's development plan, the village had a population of 221 and boasted a drug store, a grocery, and a bank.

Even as Valparaiso grew, it retained a close relationship with its sister community across the bayou. Although there had been a post office at Boggy since 1893, its name was changed to Valparaiso in 1919. When what is now Valparaiso got its own post office, it was called New Valparaiso, which only confused things. Before long, the old settlement at Boggy decided to rename its community Niceville, and New Valparaiso became Valparaiso.

John Perrine, founder of Valparaiso, and his wife, Mary, are shown in the yard of their Eastview Avenue home. Perrine had first seen this region when he camped along Tom's Bayou in 1890. Years later, he wrote, "I determined in those three never to be forgotten days . . . to some day make my home in what I knew was the real Vale of Paradise." (FSA.)

Perrine's development offered an unusual pyramid plan. Interested parties could purchase multiple lots and sell them to friends. The incentive was that they would then—theoretically—have the income from the properties they sold to cover their own living costs. (VR/WR.)

Perrine hired special railroad cars to bring interested investors down from the North. The deal he offered them was tempting—for $1,500, the purchaser got a villa lot and 10 acres of sugar cane. If the investor put $500 down, his crop could pay off the remaining $1,000! Mr. Perrine often used testimonials from satisfied customers as advertisements. One new investor, O. Stackhouse, wrote: "The villa sites at Valparaiso are the prettiest places on which to build that I have ever seen anywhere in my life. I like the climate better than California. Pure soft water, good roads, nice sociable people, no mosquitoes, very few flies, no snakes and no swamps. If there is such a thing as Paradise on earth I think I have found it." And in November of that year, the following account appeared: "My wife and I have been here for six weeks, and we have enjoyed every minute of the time. The fishing is great, bathing on our home beach is wonderful and surf bathing in the gulf is unsurpassed. The weather has been ideal. It is like June. There are now seventy-two persons living here. Everybody is happy. Watch us grow!" (HM.)

# EXTRA

## Development Necessitates the Enlargement of Original Plans

# BUSINESS LOTS

## ONE ACRE
## FIVE ACRE
## TEN ACRE

# Home Tracts

### NEXT ADJOINING AND FORMING AN EXTENSION OF THE

# Valparaiso Villa Sites

## STANDARD FARMS
### 40 Acres with 6-Room House

# Other Farm Lands
## in Walton and Okaloosa Counties

# EXTRA

City founder John Perrine constructed a large two-story frame structure at the corner of Eastview and Chicago Avenues to serve as the offices for his Valparaiso Development Company. A small company store called the Valparaiso Mercantile was at the back of the building, and the first phone exchange was located upstairs. (HM and CCB.)

As the business grew, Mr. Perrine needed to expand his offices. An addition was built onto the old building, providing him with his own office space on the second floor. He enjoyed having a view of the bayou from his new window. (HM.)

Here are some of the employees of the Valparaiso Development Company. Inside this building, loans were made to finance the purchase of homes and lots in the village. (VR/WR.)

Valparaiso is shown here in the early stages of construction. Workers are using scrapes pulled by mule teams to grade new streets. Note the Valparaiso Development Office building in the center and Mr. Perrine's personal home on the right. (HM.)

This photograph captures the view along Westview Avenue toward Tom's Bayou. Mr. Perrine's home is at the far right. (M/CCB.)

Many new residents and prospective buyers were businessmen from Chicago looking for an escape from fast-paced city life. The men shown here seem to have had a successful day of fishing with Mr. Perrine (far left). (HM.)

One of the places Mr. Perrine took his visitors was Glen Argyle. This low-lying valley was—and still is—lush with foliage. A favorite activity there was the "Trip to the Moon," a spiral stairway to the top of an 80-foot bay tree. (VR/WR.)

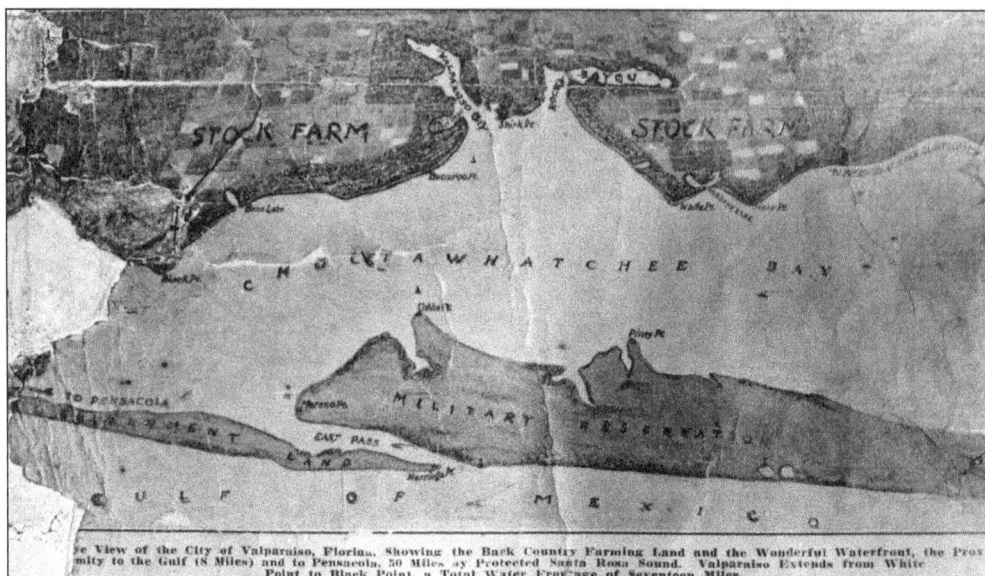

ye View of the City of Valparaiso, Florida, Showing the Back Country Farming Land and the Wonderful Waterfront, the Prox-
imity to the Gulf (8 Miles) and to Pensacola, 50 Miles by Protected Santa Rosa Sound. Valparaiso Extends from White
Point to Black Point, a Total Water Frontage of Seventeen Miles.

As part of Perrine's marketing plan, anyone who purchased a villa was offered an interest in stock farms and/or a sugar cane operation. If they bought into either investment opportunity, they were entitled to a percentage of the year's profits. (HM.)

The stock farms included a herd of 1,000 Jersey Duroc hogs. (HM.)

These visitors from the Midwest are returning to Valparaiso after a tour of the stock farm. One visitor described the scene: "The stock farm is most beautiful, lying on Rocky Bayou, and they have hundreds of acres cleared with comfortable pens, houses, etc. . . . Nearly two thousand acres of this stock farm are under fence, and everything is orderly." (HM.)

This was the dock at the stock farm. (M/CCB.)

These photographs show the cane farm operations, which were located near Freeport south of Highway 20, in 1919. The cane was processed into Paradise Syrup and was marketed not only locally, but as far away as Chicago as well. (HM and EG/WR.)

Mr. William Logan (who invested in the cane farm in 1919) wrote the following: "The cane field is a pretty sight. It stood about ten feet high and the syrup presses were turning out the juice rapidly. I saw about 2,000 gallon cans filled and ready for shipment. I also drank some of it, and it is most delicious in flavor." (M/CCB.)

According to census figures, there were 436 acres of sugarcane in production in Okaloosa County in 1920. By 1930, however, the product was not even mentioned. Cold winters or pests may have made the crop less viable. (HM.)

In this 1920s view of Westview Avenue, note construction in progress on the Valparaiso State Bank (center). (HM.)

These two homes built for the Engle family still stand today at the corner of Okaloosa and Chicago Avenues. (VR/WR.)

*Fine Boating on Valparaiso Bay Valparaiso Fla. Mar. 22 1925*

Boating has always been a popular local pastime. According to Mr. Plew, "Here you may ride for days in and out of lakes and bayous filled with luxuriant, colorful tropical foliage—down streams where giant trees draped with Spanish moss almost meet above your head. Or you may ride to Pensacola on a smooth, protected water way where Gulf storms never reach you. . . . While driving is beautiful and delightful, life at Valparaiso is scarcely complete without these alluring trips across the bay or down the bayous." (VR/WR.)

This photograph (taken in 1919) shows the wharf and warehouse Mr. Perrine installed on the shore of Tom's Bayou at the end of Westview Avenue. Boats traveled from here to Pensacola to pick up building supplies, which were then stored in this warehouse until they were used in the construction of new homes in the village. The launch *Valparaiso* is shown at the dock, the future site of Boyd's and then Spence's Boat Works. (M/CCB.)

Eventually, Capt. J. M. Jerald's launch *Grand Rapids* made two trips weekly from Pensacola to the warehouse in Valparaiso. (HM.)

*.1-1921.* *The Ferry & new Wharf at foot of E. View ave.*
*Crosses Valparaiso Bay Every 30 minutes . Fare 5¢.*

Shown here is the ferry that carried passengers from Valparaiso to Niceville in the 1920s. It left from the foot of Eastview Avenue in Valparaiso and ran every 30 minutes. In 1920, the fare across "Valparaiso Bay" (or Boggy Bayou) was a nickel. (M/CCB.)

Swearington's Boarding House was located on the corner of Westview and Glenview Avenues. When it burned, it was replaced by Morrison's Lodge, which stood for over 30 years. (HM.)

Bay Shore Hotel Valparaiso Fla.

DINNER DANCE
BAY SHORE PAVILION
NEW VALPARAISO, FLA.
SATURDAY. JULY 21
1923

Score Card

ABSENT COCKTAIL

DANCE:—INTRODUCTION FOX TROT
Please Follow Instructions of Orchestra Leader

DEEP SEA-SONED FISH

PICKLES Van Camp-Walton        SPUDS ADRIFT

DANCE:—KISS IN THE DARK

BARN YARD FLAPPER—BROILED

DEAD BEATS                SQUARE PEAS

YES WE HAVE NO BUTTER AND ROLLS

DANCE:—CONVICTS' WALTZ
Please Wear Your Number

TOMATOES A LA LONE

DANCE:—LAZY BONES

MARY ESTHER VANISHING CREAM        CAKES

This is not a prize fight—Please do not
ask for seconds

The Bayshore Hotel was built by Mr. R. A. Painter. It was located between the T-pier and the site of the Spence Brothers Boat Works along Bayshore Drive. A local newspaper reporter recorded an event there in 1919, when visitors from the North "partook of a dinner at the hotel, around a large fireplace were gathered many of the guests enjoying a pine-knot fire. . . . It seemed like a fairy story, that here in Okaloosa County, on a spot a few months ago was wilderness, was a hotel like this, surrounded by comfortable homes, more going up by the score, when flowers were in bloom, the trees were green, and the bright red holly nodded and smiled back at you a cheery welcome." When the Bayshore Hotel burned in 1921, the new and even more luxurious Valparaiso Inn was built on Bayshore Point. (M/CCB and HM.)

About 300 guests attended this New Year's Eve party at the Bayshore Hotel in 1920. (M/CCB.)

This roofed pavilion stood at the end of the long pier behind the Bayshore Hotel. Sightseeing boats took on passengers here, and at night, a live band provided music so guests could dance out over the water. (HM.)

In 1919, visitor Charles H. Lear wrote: "The children enjoy themselves immensely, bathing and playing all day long. They are not alone in this enjoyment for the adults take as great delight as they in bathing. Two and three times a day bathing suits are donned. Even in the evening one can find a group on the beach. Can northern people imagine such recreation in the middle of October?" (M/CCB.)

This photograph shows that although the planned community was only in its first stages of construction, visitors were welcomed and provided with all they would need for a pleasant stay. (Note the sign that says "Bathing Suits Rented.") The building on the left housed one of the community's first businesses, the Verbeck Store. Years later, it would become the Howell Sisters' Dress Shop, and then from 1964 to 1969, it would be part of the Okaloosa-Walton Junior College campus. (EG/WR.)

*new Valparaiso Florida*

A fascinating marketing strategy used by the Valparaiso Development Company was the production of postcards that seemed to come from an individual named "Bill Hardy." This gentleman worked for the development company, and the photos and messages on the cards were staged! This card reads: "These people make you feel at home right off. This place is even better than I thought it would be. I like it here." (VR/WR.)

*new Valparaiso Florida*

The author of this postcard writes: "Just arrived here—came by auto from Crestview—fine trip. Place looks fine to me. Hilly country. Will write more later." (VR/WR.)

Chautauqua was founded in New York State in 1874 as a summer camp for families that promised "education and uplift." The idea spread, and similar assemblies sprang up all over the country. The goal of each was to offer challenging, informational, and inspirational programs to rural and small-town America. This Florida Chautauqua was held in Perrine Park in 1921 and featured a moving-picture show followed by a dance at the Bay Shore Hotel. (HM and VR/WR.)

Before coming to Valparaiso, James Plew was a successful businessman on many fronts. He was also an ingenious inventor—he once bought a bolt of linen toweling and some wire and started a successful roller towel business. In 1897, he invented a new bicycle seat called the Plew Saddle. He also invented a drinking fountain and a hitching-post device. (HM.)

James Plew came to Valparaiso in 1922 and wrote later that "Valparaiso is the most ideal spot I have found in which to build a home." Mr. Perrine had just died, and his development company was up for sale. Plew not only took on Perrine's dream, he greatly expanded the village. He believed that Valparaiso was not a "boom town" that "relies on artificial props, or on a paper oil-well," but a "fast growing community where the foundation is laid—business and commerce grow steadily and surely along profitable but conservative lines." (EAFB.)

As part of his development plan, James Plew built a golf course. In one of his promotional brochures, he stated, "On the superb greens bordering Choctawhatchee Bay, Chicago golfers will be playing the greatest game of their lives. Twelve months each year of this, and you can have it for less than your Chicago Club dues!" Greens fees in the 1930s were $1 per day or 50¢ for nine holes. (FSA.)

Plew's brochure was written to attract the hunter as well. He states, "In the fields around Valparaiso the call of the quail is a quite familiar sound. In this picture, a big covey is being made ready for the broiler. . . . All this sport is ours for years to come because of the Florida National Reserve which surround the city, covering an area of about 422 square miles." The reserve existed as Choctawhatchee National Forest and then as the Eglin Air Force Base reservation. (FSA.)

By the time this celebration was held (just three years after development began), Mr. Plew could boast, "The Valparaiso roads are smooth and hard-surfaced. Already there are fourteen miles of them here . . . and more are being constructed as fast as material can be obtained. It is the only city in the County with electric street lights. . . . Valparaiso has its own local and long distance telephone system, and has an 8-inch self-flowing artesian well of clear, sparkling mineral water, containing many mineral elements . . . which will be disclosed when the analysis is returned by the chemist." (HM.)

# A Comet Will Hit The Earth

The latter part of June, according to astronomers. But don't let it worry you. On

## April 15th, 1921

Will occur the biggest hit of the year

### The Third Anniversary Celebration

Of the founding of

## VALPARAISO, FLORIDA

"The City Built in a Year"

### COLD DRINKS, LUNCHES

A hundred Amusements

Come and enjoy the time of your life

## Valpariso Inn

### for

## Winter Guests

Desiring a
Semi-tropical
Climate

—◆—

### Steam Heated
Throughout

Log Burning Fireplace

—◆—

### Moderate Temperature

for

Hunting
Fishing
Golf
Tennis
Motoring and
Boating

## Valpariso Inn

### for

## Summer Guests

Desiring the Cool
Breezes of
Choctawhatchee Bay
and the
Gulf of Mexico

Spacious Verandas
on Three Floors

White Sand Bathing Beach

Diving Platform
for Swimmers

Two Tennis Courts
on Hotel Grounds

Boating and Sport Fishing
in Salt and Fresh Water and
in the Gulf of Mexico

The luxurious Valparaiso Inn, patterned after a famous Chicago establishment, the Edgewater Beach Hotel, was built by James Plew in 1924. It was advertised as having 56 "thoroughly modern" rooms, boasted a grand ballroom on the third floor and a "roof garden," and was located just 40 yards from the shore of the bayou. (CB and HM.)

The Inn
VALPARAISO
FLORIDA

CORNER OF LIVING ROOM

An article in the *Pensacola Journal* at the time describes the interior: "The interior of the hotel in two-toned walnut . . . with hardwood floors . . . and the furniture and lights were purchased with a view to harmonizing with the interior decorative scheme." (HM.)

TENNIS COURT VALPARISO INN GROUNDS VALPARISO, FLA.

B-214

Trainloads of visitors from Chicago would come to the inn to enjoy tennis and horseback riding. (VR/WR.)

Many of them would just relax on the porch. (HM.)

This woman is standing in the yard of the inn, pictured with a loggerhead turtle. Apparently, these large turtles captured the attention of early visitors just as they do today. The loggerhead has lost much of its nesting habitat due to the recent development of our beaches and is now considered an endangered species. (HM.)

The inn accommodated potential buyers, vacationers, and military personnel over the years. Members of the Ruckel family recall hosting parties at the inn for the men who trained with Jimmy Doolittle for his raid on Tokyo. Dancing, entertainment, and "Special Sunday Dinners" were just some of the activities that occurred there. The inn remained the center of social life in the village for many years. (CB.)

The inn was converted to apartments in 1956. It burned in 1977 and again, for the last time, in 1980, just after it had been listed on the National Register of Historic Places. (HM.)

Not only did Mr. Plew construct home sites in the village; he also ensured the long-term success of his community by encouraging business establishments. In addition to the small stores shown in this photograph, he built the Valparaiso State Bank, seen just left of center. Valparaiso also had a pulp mill, a concrete brick plant, and an ice factory. The Valparaiso business district is shown above in 1931. (HM.)

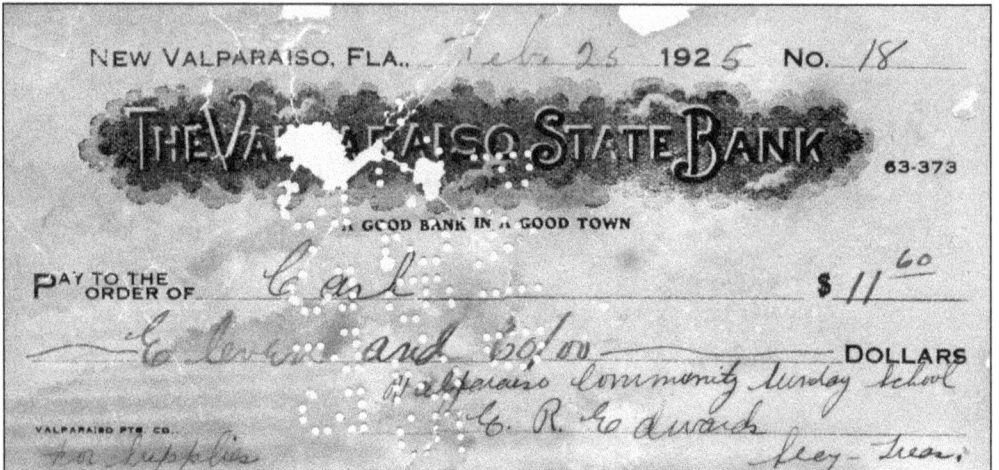

This was the Valparaiso Hardware Store in the 1920s and 1930s, then Brabham's Drycleaners, and finally the Howell Sisters' Dress Shop. (VR/WR.)

As the village grew, the Valparaiso Telephone Exchange moved from the development office to this building. (EG/WR.)

James Plew donated land for a church in Valparaiso, and construction began on the Community Church in 1925. Charter members included James and Nettie Plew, Addie Lewis, J. P. and Hannah Nordberg, and Mr. and Mrs. Ed Freiwald. In the 1930s, pastors from different denominations were brought in to conduct services. When the collection plate did not produce $8 to pay the minister, Mrs. Plew made up the difference. In 1936, the church acquired its first full-time clergyman, Dr. Frank Fox, and the Plews donated a house next to the church for a parsonage. (HM.)

One unique fund-raiser to support church work was organized in 1919: an Old Maids Sale! The unmarried women of the village were covered with a sheet and offered to the highest bidder, with all proceeds going to the church. Would-be purchasers were reminded that "when a girl reaches 18 she is considered an old maid in Valparaiso." Although the church has changed denominations over the years, it has continuously served as a spiritual center for local residents. (HM.)

Valparaiso's first developer, John Perrine, considered education a priority, and so he built a one-story frame building for the purpose in 1921. The building contained grades one through eight and served children from both Valparaiso and Niceville. The school was also the location of occasional fund-raisers, such as cakewalks, to raise money for church work and "for feeding the hungry across the sea." (HM.)

The Valparaiso School student body is pictured here in 1921. (HM.)

Students at the Valparaiso School are pictured here in the 1930s. The students identified here are, from left to right, (first row) Elaine Windom Alford, Louise Johnson Kelly, Talmadge Spencer Hart, Naomi Allen Hicks, Laura Brown Regans, and Epsie Willingham Killen. (HM.)

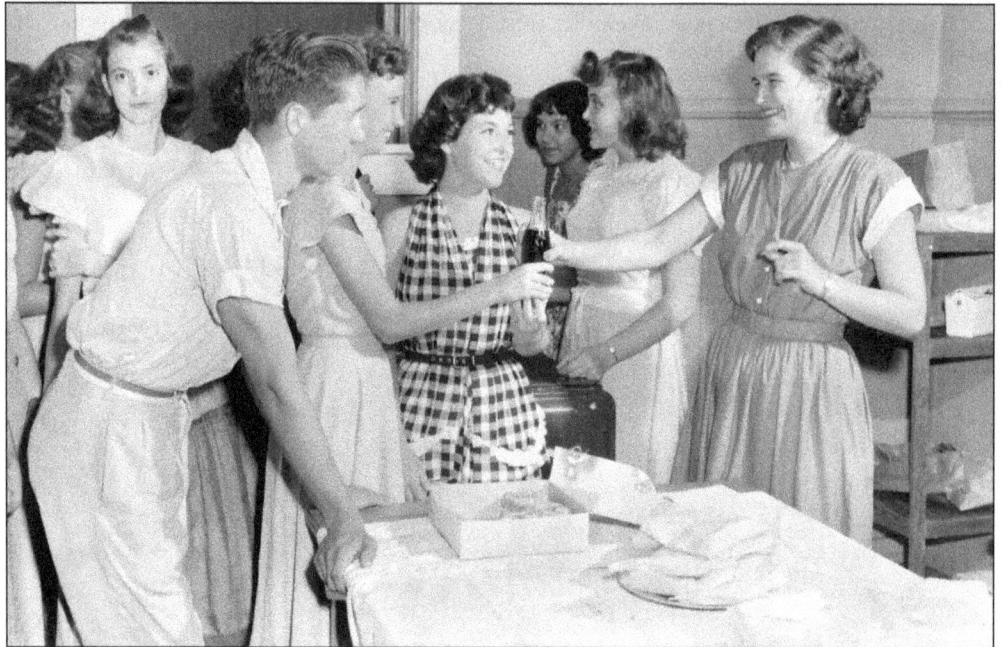

In 1941, the building was purchased by the City of Valparaiso, and in the years that followed, it was used as a community center, a youth center, and a physical education facility for the community college. The Niceville High School Seniors Club is shown here at the center in 1951. In 1989, the city commission, planning board, and public works department worked together to renovate and repair the structure. Today it serves as the local senior center and remains a center of activity in the village. (CB.)

After the Valparaiso Development Company was sold to Mr. Plew, its former offices were modified. Jane Lewis Phillips's grandparents ran a grocery store there, and she remembers that the candy counter was on the right and dry goods on the left side of store, while vegetables and fruit were farther back. The meat market, managed by her father, was located in the rear. Her father, Vernon Lewis, traveled all around the area buying sausage, poultry, rabbit, cold cuts, and rounds of cheese. (VR/WR.)

In the 1940s, Harry Reynolds opened the Valparaiso Store on the corner of Westview and Chicago Avenues. In the 1950s, it was taken over by Mack Mitchell. Locals remember that there was no air conditioning in the store, and a large fan just inside would not only circulate the air but would also quickly rearrange their hair! Many learned to stoop as they entered and cover their heads with their hands to minimize the damage. Favorite purchases included meat from Sleepy the butcher, Rocky Bayou eggs, and hoop cheese. (VR/WR.)

Downtown Valparaiso in the early 1950s included the Valparaiso State Bank, Mitchell's Hardware Store, and Mitchell's Market/Grocery. (CB.)

Started by the federal government in 1942 as a clinic, this facility was purchased by the City of Valparaiso five years later for the establishment of a community hospital. Fashion shows, dinners, and a raffle were held to raise funds for a renovation, including the installation of an operating room. When a new hospital was built in Niceville in 1963, this facility was closed and was re-opened as a science building for the community college. Returning to its roots, today the old hospital houses the offices of several local physicians. (CB.)

In 1952, the Valparaiso Fire Department purchased its first truck. Known affectionately as "Old Betsy," the truck still serves as a reserve pumper and hose tender. Before 1952, the department relied on a two-wheel hose cart that would be pulled to a hydrant by two men. Because most homes were located between the bayous in old Valparaiso, the cart was stored in a shed at the Valparaiso Inn. (VFD.)

When a fire call came in to the station, the engine would move through town slowly so that shopkeepers and other businessmen who were volunteer firemen could run outside and jump on. Anyone who missed the truck could go to the station and read the address of the fire on the blackboard there. Many members of the community would go to the fires to help move hoses or carry furniture out of burning buildings. (VFD.)

The neighborhood grocery store, Piggly Wiggly, shown *c.* 1951, was located at the intersection of Highways 20 and 190. This was the beginning of the move from the old downtown to what is now John Sims Parkway. (CB.)

In 1952, the Board of Directors of the Valparaiso State Bank authorized the construction of a new facility, to be built right next to the old one. At this time, the facility offered a new convenience—a drive-through window. Traffic along Westview Avenue would soon diminish, however, with the completion of the new four-lane John Sims Parkway, and the bank would relocate to the corner of John Sims and Edge Avenue. (The original two-story brick bank building was razed in 1976. The second bank building now houses the Heritage Museum of Northwest Florida, and the third location is now Vanguard Bank.) (VB.)

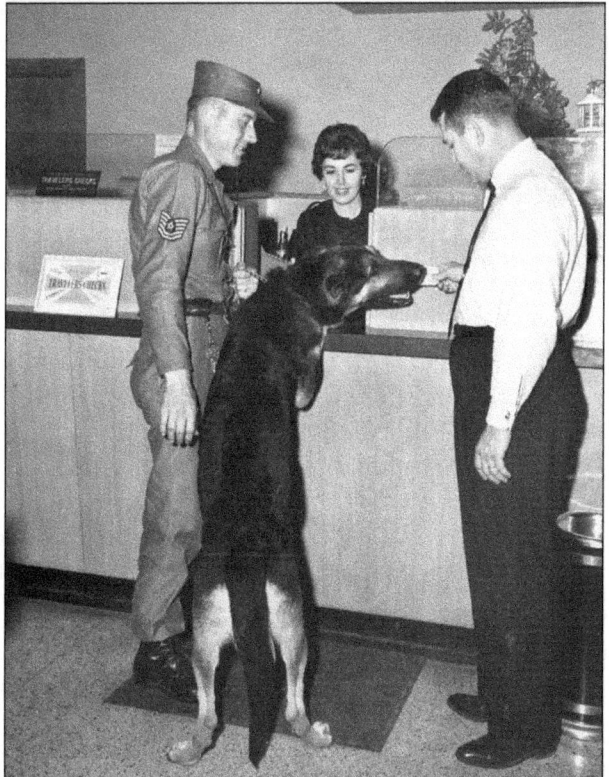

"We welcome every depositor!" Norma Hoyle and Randy Roberts accept a deposit from an Eglin security officer and his dog, Midnight, in 1957. (VB.)

97

When two-lane Forrest Avenue became four-lane John Sims Parkway in 1961, development on the previously undeveloped site of the parkway resulted in a major shift of business away from the old downtown. Shops closed, so when the new Okaloosa-Walton Junior College expressed interest in leasing out the old downtown, the city agreed. Valparaiso became known as "the city that became a college." The old Morrison's Lodge served as student center, and the Valparaiso State Bank became the liberal arts building. Carter's Jewelry Store was the library, the Howell Sisters' Apparel and Beauty Shop was the student faculty center, and Bay Hospital was used for physical education. (CB.)

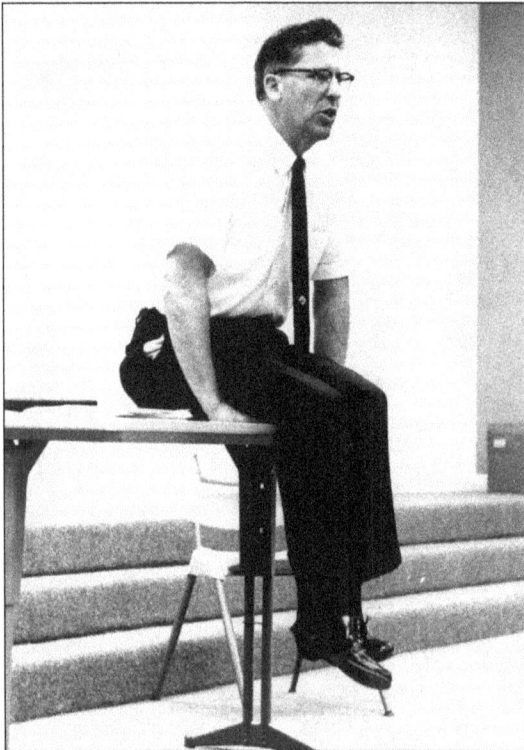

Dr. James E. McCracken was the first president of the college, and he continued to serve as such for 24 years. In the early days of the college, Dr. James and Mrs. Ruth McCracken opened their home on Sunday afternoons to the entire student body. They would set up board games and have a cookout on the lawn. (JMc.)

Mannings Bar and Café, shown here in 1945, was located on the water side of John Sims Parkway near the boundary of Niceville and Valparaiso. Note the sign on the right: "Plate lunch 35¢." (CB.)

In the 1930s, Mr. Findley Duncan (of Duncan Amusements) built this structure so that he could store his inventory of game and cigarette machines. As his business grew, he moved to other locations and rented the front of this building to other tenants. In the 1950s, Mr. Hobbs ran a feed store here, and later a car repair shop occupied the building. Today it houses Country Corners Discount Tires. (CV.)

This 1940s aerial view illustrates how little development had taken place in Valparaiso prior to World War II. During and after the war, additional housing was constructed for air force personnel, and when Highway 20 was widened to four lanes, development increased on the north side of the road. One of the most interesting features of this photo is the cattle fence, which was installed in the 1920s and ran along Highway 20 from Tom's Bayou to Niceville. Cattle gaps (or guards) were installed on Bay Shore Drive and on Seminole and Okaloosa Avenues to keep livestock from entering the residential area. (CB.)

# Five

# FISHING AND BOATING

The first commercial industries of any size along the bayou were sawmills and turpentine stills, but from the very beginning, almost everyone fished.

According to most accounts, the first in the region to fish with a net was Aaron Howell, who sold his catch from a mule-driven wagon. Ida Coon remembers when "Every year, farmers from Alabama would come down to the coast to buy a load of fish. We could always tell when they had sold their cotton. They'd put some greenbacks in their pocket and come down in their wagons or oxcarts to buy a mess of fish. They were only three cents a pound back then. They put those fish to pickle so they wouldn't spoil, but after they soaked them and cooked 'em they tasted good."

Real commercial fishing began just after the turn of the 20th century when young Claude Meigs (who brought his bride, Cebelle Warren, from DeFuniak Springs to Boggy Bayou) started to buy fish (mostly mullet) from other fisherman and then sell them in Alabama. Eventually he opened the Niceville Fish Company, where fish were salted, packed in barrels, and shipped to other markets.

During the Depression, the Spence family closed down their sawmill and started a dairy operation on their farm. When it became difficult to buy feed for their cows, they bought mullet from local fishermen too, and then traded it to farmers in the northern part of the county for feed. This operation grew, and in the 1940s, they bought out Claude Meigs. Their small plant, located on Bayshore Drive, eventually grew into an international business.

Not only did the waters provide food for the table, but, according to Walker Spence, "We didn't have much recreation, [so] we mainly fished. This bay [the Choctawhatchee] and all these bayous were brackish waters. There was plenty of fresh water fishin'. When I was a kid you could go anywhere and catch as many fresh water fish as you wanted." (EAFB.)

Samuel Lancaster's fish house, located near present-day Rocky Bayou Bridge, operated in the late 19th century. Lancaster and his family made their own fishing nets and fished from open skiffs. They would pole the boat along the shore until they spotted fish and then would pull a seine net around them, trapping them between the net and the beach. (GEC.)

102

The commercial seafood industry was first developed in 1918 by Niceville resident Claude Meigs, who started the Bayou Fish Company. He renamed the business the Niceville Fish Company. Thirty-three years later, this business was bought by Walter and Wallace Spence, and Mr. Meigs went into the construction business to provide homes for the many military families coming in to serve at Eglin Air Force Base. The bridge across Rocky Bayou is named after Mr. Meigs. (CPP and HM.)

CLAUDE MEIGS          CLIFFORD MEIGS

# NICEVILLE FISH CO

RED SNAPPER—GROUPER—SPANISH MACKEREL
POMPANO—BLUE FISH AND OTHER VARIETIES

We handle from one to two million pounds of fish annually and our twenty years experience in the business have taught us how to give prompt and reliable service on all orders from one pound to a car load.

The *Lucky Strike*, an early line-fishing boat, was used to catch snapper, grouper, warsaw, and other kinds of fish. It was owned by Tellor Howell and captained by Benny Allen. Tellor's father, Aaron Howell, introduced houseboat-style bay boats to Boggy. (TR.)

Melvin Allen and young Jim Hicks are in the snapper boat *Bob*. The Hicks family has always been known for their skill as commercial fishermen. They still ply the local waters in their boat *Family Pride*. (WH.)

Frank Reynolds (on right) is shown here in 1940 with his prize catch, a world-record snapper. The fish weighed 114.5 pounds. Wallace Spence (left) and Mac Logan (center) look on. (CSA/CB.)

105

The Spence brothers first operated the Spence Brothers Fish Company on Highway 20, near where the Spence Apfel Office is today. After losing two buildings to fire, they relocated to Claude Meigs's old store on Bayshore Drive in Niceville. Eventually they moved to a new location just down the street and remained there until they closed in 1996. Their fishing fleet plied the waters of the Gulf of Mexico for long-line bottom fish such as snapper, grouper, warsaw, and scamp. They often returned with thousands of pounds of fish. This company provided fish to markets around the world. Hanging in the background behind Walter (left) and Wallace are two king mackerel, two red snapper, a warsaw, and a grouper. (CSA/CB and HM.)

106

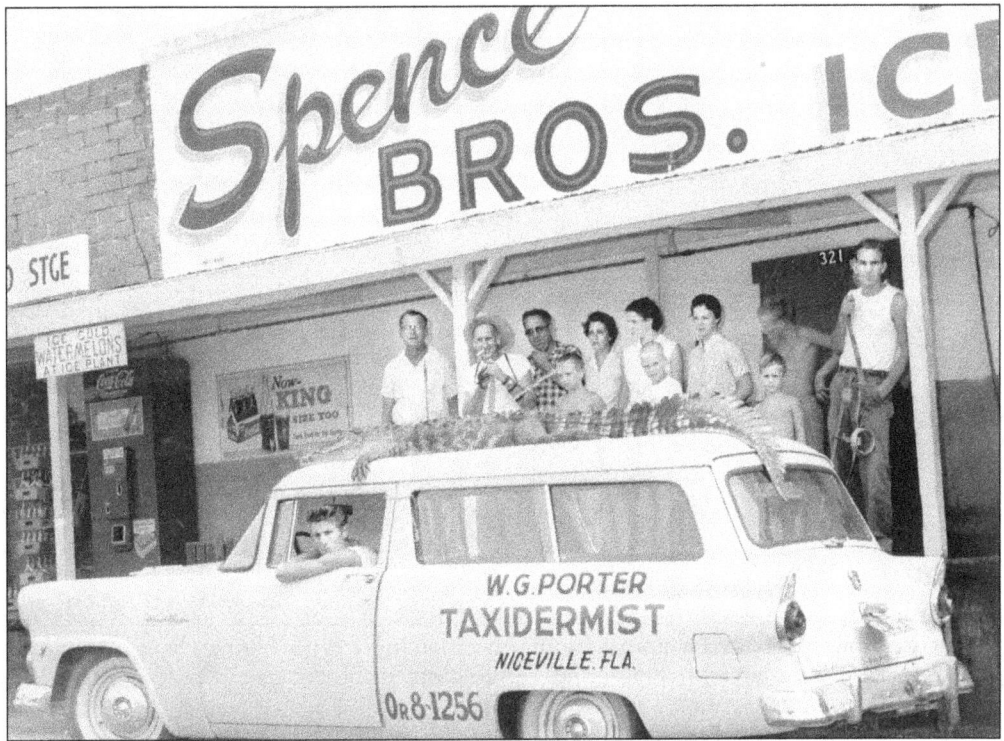

This is a different kind of catch! Taken in 1958, this photograph shows Dan Hatchett (standing second from the left) with the alligator he, R. J. Kelly, and Glen Porter killed in Choctawhatchee Bay just off Rocky Bayou. The alligator measured seven feet long, and it reportedly took six arrows to stop him. (CSA.)

Ice had been available locally in small quantities since the 1920s, but commercial fishing required tons of it. The Davis Ice Plant, co-owned by Tilly and Davis, was next door to the fish house. Twenty-four hours a day, it produced block ice, using ammonia as the freezing agent. Excess ice was dumped into the bayou. This site had previously been the location of the first local power plant, which furnished power as far away as Fort Walton Beach. It was eventually sold to Gulf Power. (CN.)

This scene shows Mr. Willingham's bay fishing operation in Niceville. His nets have been placed on a reel next to a freshwater stream so they can be cleaned. Other nets can be seen on the left, hung from poles along the water's edge to dry. (TR.)

Bud Parish is shown here holding a 35-pound red fish that was caught in his shrimp net. His net was the type first used on the bayou in the 1950s and had to be pulled out of the water by hand. Later boats had a winch for this purpose. (JP.)

During the 1970s and 1980s, the shrimp industry grew, and local boats began to go into the Gulf of Mexico. In the 1990s, net bans and worldwide competition discouraged local shrimpers, and only a few continue. Shown here at the peak of the local industry, each of these vessels would be loaded with fuel, ice, and enough groceries to feed four or five men for 15 to 20 days. Shrimp would be hauled aboard, picked out, and their heads removed. They were packed in ice in the hold to stay fresh until they reached the market. (CB.)

During the Depression, most families owned "bay boats," which were used for both fishing and recreation. Boat building was a natural outgrowth of the fishing industry, and for years, men built their own boats in their backyards. Ansley Edge, a Niceville mullet fisherman, is shown here in the 1940s putting the finishing touches on a skiff that he will pull behind his bay boat. The skiff will be used to hold his nets. (GEC.)

The Parish Boat Works, located just south of Lions Park, was established by George Parish in the 19th century. He built sailing ships that were known throughout the Southeast. The last boat produced by this boat works was built by Bud Parish in the 1960s. Today Mr. Parish builds detailed models of the boats that came from local boat works. (CSA.)

This boat works, located at Gray Moss Point in Niceville, was started by the Parish brothers in the early 20th century. James Parish Sr. and John Robert (Bob) Parish were taught shipbuilding skills by their grandfather. The boat in this photograph was a shrimp boat named *Magic City*, built by James Parish Jr. (JP.)

The *Regina* was built at Parish Boat Works. It was bought by the Luthrams for use as a pleasure boat. (JP.)

In many cases, boats were named after family members to honor them. This was true for the *Isaac S. Boles*. Benton Boles had the boat built and named it after his father. Columbus Thompson and Martin Hudson built the boat in 1940. They used a combination of pine, juniper, and cypress wood in the construction. One technique to bend the planks covering the hull was to use a steam vat to make them pliable. (CB.)

The *Isaac S. Boles* was initially configured with a diesel engine for primary power and two masts and sails for secondary power. The crew used hand lines for catching fish. (CSA.)

Boyd's Auto and Boat Works Garage offered many services, such as welding, machine work, boat storage, and small-boat building. It was located in Valparaiso at New Point Comfort. The Spence family took over the operation in the 1950s. Employees for the Spence Brothers Boat Works shown here from left to right in 1943 are Martin Hudson, Burroughs Hicks, Columbus Thompson, John Boyd, Robert Patterson, Wilber Senterfitt, Fitzhugh Gunnels, and Charles Rogers. (CSA.)

Boyd's Boat Works, shown here, eventually became Spence Brothers Boat Works. When the marine boatways (visible here) were added, wooden boats could be pulled up on land for repair. (CSA.)

This is the water-side view of the Spence Brothers Boat Works, where boats were cleaned and/or repaired. To the far left are the rental boat slips. The boats at the dock are part of the family's snapper fleet, including the S. S. Spence, named by the brothers to honor their father. A bay boat is tied up to the dock beside it. Most of the Spence family fishing fleet was built at the boat works. This facility was destroyed by fire in 1997. (CB and JG.)

*Six*

# EGLIN AIR FORCE BASE
## *The Military Comes to Town*

In the 1930s, pilots from Maxwell Field, an Army Air Corps training ground in nearby Alabama, often flew from Montgomery to Valparaiso for long weekends to golf and fish. When the commanding officer of Maxwell Field initiated action to secure a gunnery and bombing range for the tactical school based at the field, local residents affected by the Depression realized the economic possibilities of having a base in their midst. In an effort to encourage officials to locate the range here, James Plew built two landing strips, which he then called the Valparaiso Airport. Soon the CCC cleared more land, and the airport facility was enlarged and improved. To this day, the original Valparaiso Airport and its runways accommodate both military and commercial air traffic.

In 1934, James Plew donated 1,460 acres to the federal government to establish a full-scale military reservation, and the Valparaiso Airport was renamed the Valparaiso Bombing and Gunnery Base. In 1937, the base was renamed Eglin Field to honor Lt. Col. Frederick I. Eglin, a Maxwell pilot who had been killed in a plane crash that year.

As the threat of war loomed on the horizon, officials considered enlarging the base by transferring Choctawhatchee National Forest over to Eglin Field. Local opinion was divided: landowners within the forest feared their property would be confiscated, and hunters and fisherman were loath to give up access to their favorite haunts. Newspapers, business leaders, and local politicians supported the expansion and believed the economic benefit would far outweigh any loss or inconvenience. Valparaiso mayor C. W. Ruckel, James Plew's son-in-law, went so far as to say that the expansion of Eglin Field was the "rainbow which we are all chasing."

Choctawhatchee National Forest officially became part of Eglin Field in 1940. Since then, Eglin has become the largest air force base in the U.S. Department of Defense. From World War II through Korea, Vietnam, and more recent conflicts, Eglin personnel have designed and tested some of the most effective weaponry in existence.

Servicing planes at gunnery camp.

When the Valparaiso Airport first became the landing strip for the new Valparaiso Bombing and Gunnery Base in 1935, water had to be brought in by the barrel and enlisted men slept on cots on the porches of the yet-to-be-finished barracks. Discipline was lax—men only worked four days a week—and the site continued to be seen as a place to relax. But as World War II loomed ever closer, the base saw more action as increasing numbers of pilots arrived there for training. (HM and EAFB.)

ARMY AIR PORT EGLIN FIELD VALPARISO, FLA.

A transient camp had been established at White Point in 1934, designed to provide employment for those who "drift into the state and who find themselves stranded without employment or a place of abode. Its personnel is a changing one as the men comprising it are given opportunity at regular periods of being returned to their former homes." About 240 Depression-era workers were initially brought in to work on the new air field. The community at large benefited from their presence, too—they worked on other projects such as paving new roadways and stringing a telephone line to Valparaiso. The camp was eventually turned over to the Maxwell Field Officer's Club for use as a holiday camp. (FSA.)

In 1935, a newspaper reporter named the Valparaiso Airport "among the best." "The field includes 1440 acres, and is built to permit planes to land and take off from any direction. It is considered by many competent observers to be among the two or three best fields in the state. A detachment of men and officers from Maxwell Field is on duty at the field, and this force will be enlarged considerably when additional facilities are provided." Depression relief agencies would soon provide funds and labor to pave the runways and build offices, barracks, and other buildings as needed. The salvage yard at Maxwell Field also provided materials for the new base: latrines were flown down from there in a C-14. (EAFB.)

The *Valparaiso News* reported by 1936, "Much progress has been made on the construction of buildings. . . . An Army field radio has been installed and daily radio communication with Maxwell Field is held. . . . Nine tents have been erected at the airport and to accommodate a number of men who have been arriving during the last few days." (EAFB.)

During World War II, this area suffered an extreme housing shortage as the base population increased rapidly at Eglin. Charles Ruckel, James Plew's son-in-law, established the Valparaiso Homes Corporation and built a number of new two-bedroom homes for the servicemen and their families. These homes have affectionately become known as "Ruckel Houses." Ruckel is shown here with his daughter, Rae. (WR.)

This boathouse was located just across Tom's Bayou from New Point Comfort. It was built by the military to store crash boats, which were used to tow targets and to recover planes and pilots that crashed into the bay. The crew lived the quarters on the second floor. (HM.)

The air force base has occasionally provided an exciting moment, when one of the many planes flying overhead has met with a malfunction. This photograph shows a plane that went down on Edge Avenue in 1941. Overall, however, the safety record at Eglin has been exemplary, and citizens are hardly aware of the constant testing that goes on within its boundaries. (WR.)

The Boy Scout Camp at Eglin Air Force Base has been active for over 60 years. During the late 1940s and into the 1950s, an Air Scout Group was created for older boys. They learned about aircraft types, theories of flight, and other aviation-related topics. (NP.)

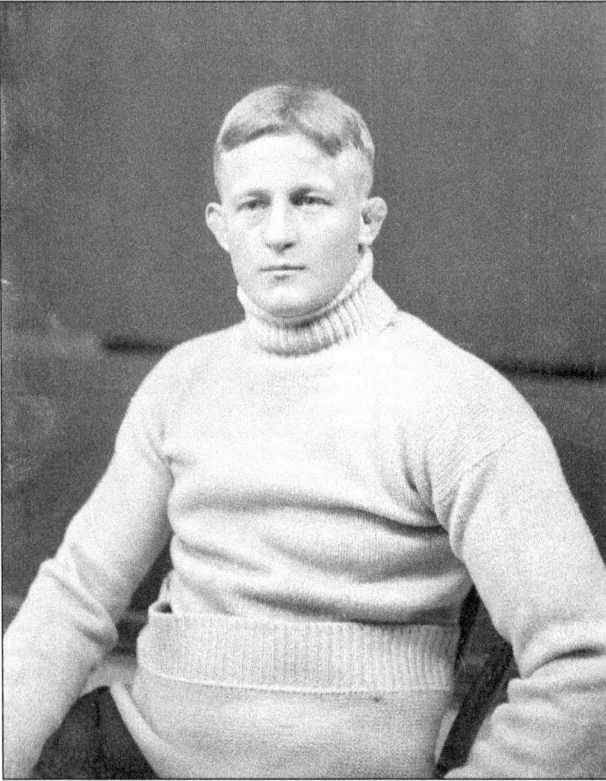

Mr. Charlie Postl, an immigrant from Austria, established the first commercial health and fitness club in Chicago in 1908. He had become friends with Teddy Roosevelt, and a few years later, when Postl's partner absconded with the club's funds, Roosevelt allowed his name to be used in an advertisement for the club. Apparently this was the first time any living former president's picture and endorsement had been used in this way. The advertisement helped the club through a hard time, but so did the growing public awareness that "fit was better than fat." (CHS.)

In 1926, Mr. Postl purchased land across Tom's Bayou from Valparaiso (a location that eventually became part of Eglin AFB) and started Postl's Haven, a fitness lodge and resort. Many major-league baseball players at the time frequented Postl's Chicago club, and it was hoped that they would come to Valparaiso and establish a regular training camp here. (VR/CCB.)

Plans called for a two-story, 52-room structure patterned after the existing Valparaiso Inn. It was to be topped by a lighted glass dome that would be seen for miles—even from the Gulf of Mexico! There was to be a recreation building with mineral baths, rubbing slabs, and quarters for the masseurs. An enclosed heated pool was also planned, to be kept at 76 degrees year-round. Outdoor facilities would include gym equipment, running tracks, trap-shooting grounds, putting greens, and an archery range. Horses and boats would be available to guests, too. (HM.)

Advertisements for the club read: "Postl's Gulf Coast Club: Who enters here leaves care behind; who lingers, joy of health will find." Apparently, the Depression ended Mr. Postl's dream. In 1935, Louie "Two Gun" Arterie, a Chicago gang leader, was planning to buy the place and turn it into a gambling palace. After returning to Chicago from Pensacola, however, he was gunned down as he stepped out of his apartment. After the military took over the land, the clubhouse was used by Eglin personnel as a service club. One account states that the building was eventually destroyed by fire. (HM.)

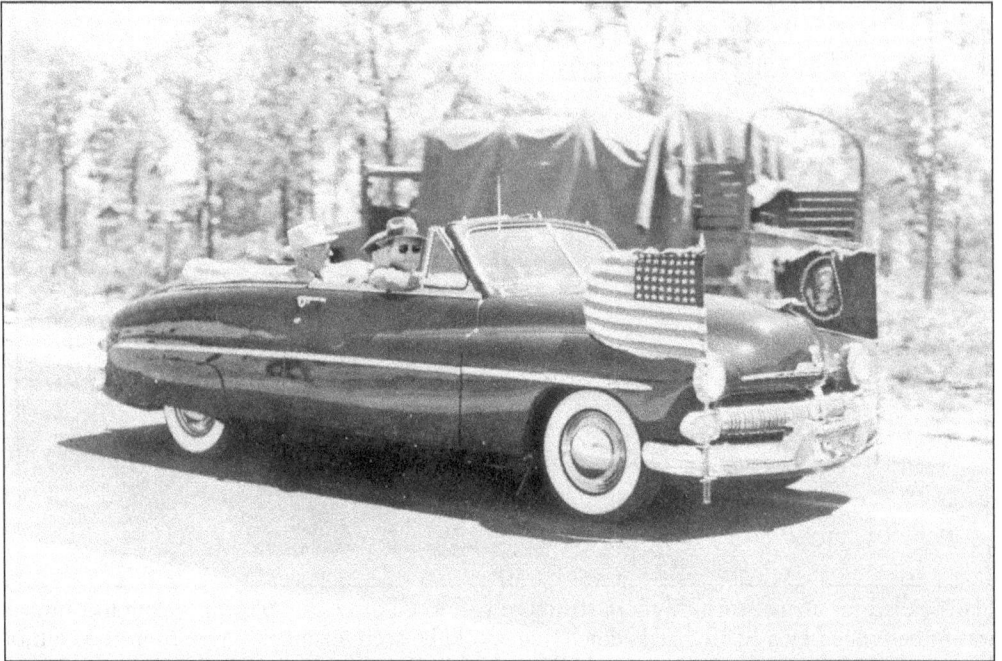

The presence of Eglin AFB has brought famous visitors to the twin cities. In 1950, Pres. Harry Truman came to attend a firepower demonstration of both propeller- and jet-powered aircraft. Many government officials were invited to attend. Gen. Omar Bradley, chairman of the joint chiefs of staff, was one of them. (HM.)

In 1962, Pres. John F. Kennedy attended a similar demonstration, and an estimated 30,000 people lined the parade route to catch a glimpse of the popular president. The *Bayou Gazette* reported, "The Presidential Party . . . was hailed by crowds along the roads, atop cars and homes and from numerous water craft and party fishing boats in the bayous." (HM.)

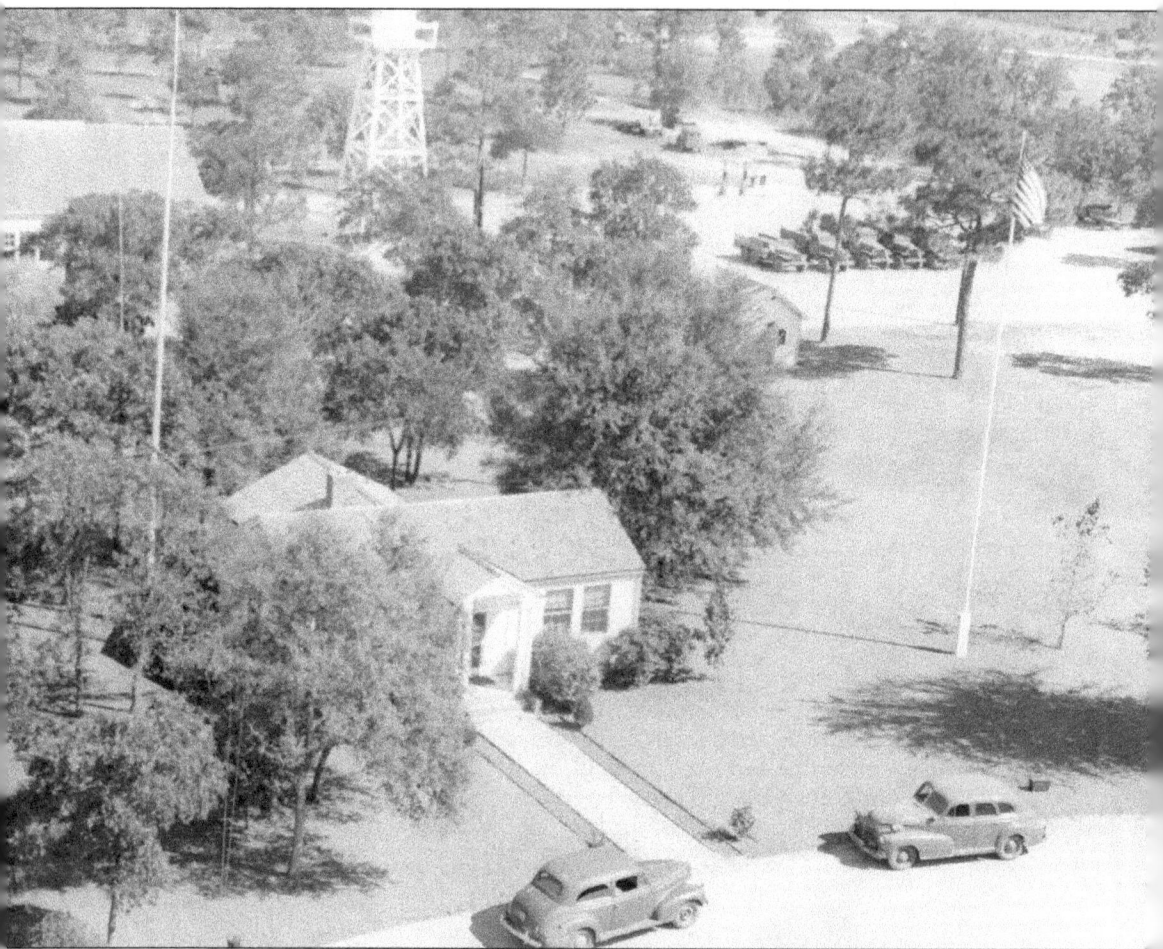

The Jackson Guard Office, shown here, was built in 1937. Thanks to the commitment of the U.S. Air Force at Eglin to natural resource conservation, the region once known as Choctawhatchee National Forest retains one of the few remaining stands of longleaf pines. This effort, in turn, provides habitat for the endangered red-cockaded woodpecker. Other threatened species, such as the burrowing owl and the loggerhead turtle, are also monitored and protected by Eglin's natural resources branch, Jackson Guard, which manages the forests and issues public permits for hunting, fishing, hiking, and so forth within the boundaries of the reservation. Without the vast, government-controlled band of green space that forms a semi-circle around the Twin Cities, the communities would likely have experienced much more urban sprawl and, in the process, lost their small-town charm. (Fr S.)

# EPILOGUE

The communities between the bayous are still known for extending a warm welcome to visitors seeking respite from the cold and to military families who come and go as their assignments direct them. And because life is good here, many who thought only to pass through will decide to stay.

There is no denying that these communities have grown and changed since their beginnings, and yet, if you ask them, residents of Valparaiso will still tell you they believe they have found the "Vale of Paradise" and folks in Niceville will tell you that living there is "just plain nice."

The Twin Cities region offers an excellent quality of life, partly because of the moderate climate and partly because the recreational opportunities that lured those early investors to this region are still here today. The area boasts excellent schools, several college campuses, and a few museums that strive to preserve the region's rich cultural past. Jackson Guard and other local conservationist groups continue to ensure the protection of our unique natural resources.

This will always be a special place. As James Plew once wrote, "Away from the rush and roar of the city—away from strife and care—far from the frozen winters, the stifling summers of the north—Here we will live in joyous freedom under our own 'vine and fig tree!' "

This local landmark, which sits at the head of Boggy Bayou, perfectly captures the atmosphere in and around the Twin Cities: "Nice Folks," "Nice Town," "Have a Nice Time!" (BB.)